KINGSTON BUTTERCUP

# ACKNOWLEDGEMENTS

Special thank you to Jeremy Poynting, Kwame Dawes, Hannah Bannister and Adam Lowe at Peepal Tree Press for their patience, keen eyes and big hearts.

Thank you to the following journals and anthologies that have graciously featured some of the poems in their earlier forms: *Bim; The Caribbean Writer; Jamaica Journal;* the anthology *Tough Times in America; WomanSpeak: A Journal of Literature and Art by Caribbean Women,* and the Bookends literary pull-out of the *Jamaica Observer*.

In addition to being published in *Jamaica Journal*, "Bearing Witness", the ode to Jamaican Poet Laureate, appeared on the King's House and Institute of Jamaica websites, to mark the inauguration of Jamaica's Poet Laureate.

Thank you to poets Mervyn Morris, Eddie Baugh, Earl McKenzie, Loretta Collins Klobah, Safiya Sinclair, Millicent Graham, Olive Senior, Ishion Hutchinson, Valzyna Mort and the late Wayne Brown – friends, mentors, role models.

Remembering all poets, living and deceased, who've inspired, including, of course, Bob Marley!

ANN-MARGARET LIM

KINGSTON BUTTERCUP

PEEPAL TREE

First published in Great Britain in 2016
Peepal Tree Press Ltd
17 King's Avenue
Leeds LS6 1QS
UK

ISBN 13: 9781845233303

Supported using public funding by
**ARTS COUNCIL
ENGLAND**

# CONTENTS

# SPIRIT TREES

In memory of Mary Suen Chin;
for Oswald Lim, Kayla Kerr
and the family in all its locations.

## AND THEY INHABIT THE LANDSCAPE STILL

The nodding grass, with its silk-lavender,
purple-red antennae,
dreams me a Taino in his canoe
paddling to his woman,
and her swinging
in a cotton hammock
with a Taino and his canoe on her mind.

The sound of traffic
trailing the contours of this hill
tells of the approaching tumult
of horseborne men.

# ECHOES IN THE BONE: TESTIMONIALS

*Before I be a slave, I'll skip over my grave
and go home to my Fadder and be free.*
— Clancy Eccles

*I: High School Girl*:

Under the poinciana
on the bench at school,
my eye surveys the unlevelled field,
the unpainted wall
separating one school from another,

and goosebumps come
as the ancestors tell
how the rickety wooden boxes
we use for club meetings
remind of their living quarters –
thatched roofs in lieu of wood;

how below the staffroom
was the black room
they were thrown in.

*II: Pregnant Woman*:

Driving through a cane piece
in St. Catherine at night,
the ancestors tell me
of a storm of backra massas
flattening the grass girls in the fields.

As my guts spew,
a line of Royal Palms reminds
of the Great House above,
the bend of the black neck below.

# ON READING THISTLEWOOD'S DIARY

*The songs of the slave represent the sorrows of his heart; and he is
relieved by them, only as an aching heart is relieved by its tears.*
— Frederick Douglass

I

Livestock hamstrung, lamed, missing,
back broken, thrown off a cliff;
Massa's transport slashed in the belly, gut hanging;
potato slips planted wrong;
machetes with their own minds
mutilating human cattle;
the spit-seasoned soup, coffee, tea;
black men and women walking into drownings;
repeatedly running,
refusing to spread the legs,
braving the bilboes, a lashing,
the dungeon, a branding;
killing the whiteman, braving a hanging

– resistance in miserable slavery.

II

Susanna, dat's ma name.
Don't confuse it wid de open-air African savannah.
If yu look mi up *In Miserable Slavery*
you'll si mi listed under children,
wid Congo in bracket, page 29.

Ah was part o' de pickney gang in 1751
when him firs' tek mi
in de curing house.

Ah wet him bed him tek mi in.
Each time ah wet de bed,
but him neva stop.

An' yu, who fin' him diary an' call mi favourite,
tell de worl' how dem whip mi an Mazerine
for refusing backra an' him fren;

tell di worl' how T'istlewood
an' slavery ruin mi.


III

Dear Phibbah,

Your name half-rhymes with Syvah –
the dance move that's in.
So when I think of you, I say,
*Syvah, syvah, syvah*, like in the song,
and you know, Phibbah, it's not a bad comparison,
for when women syvah, they squat for takeoff,
spread wings and fly.

When they syvah, Phibbah,
their feet remember
the wheels and tuns you did
at fellow slaves' wakes,
singing, *When I die hallelujah bye, bye
I'll fly away*.

And the takeoff,
when the body comes fully into play,
is the throwing off of shackles,
and I sing: *Syvah, syvah, syvah,*
and think of you, Phibbah,
in miserable slavery.

How you suffered through each infection
Thistlewood gave you
as he cummed every skirt it crossed his mind to fuck;
how you must have wailed when his son –
your mulatto child died.
This wasn't in the diary. He kept it 'dignified'.
And as the women release in
*syvah, syvah, syvah*,
their hands like albatross' wings,
I think: *Phibbah, in what moment*
*did you hatch your freedom plan*
*on this confounded man?*


IV

Descending Red Hills in the morning
I think: this is not so different
from what Thistlewood saw –

the same green from the trees;
the air blanketed with lingering sleep;
caterpillars of smoke crawling up the sky.

Walking the streets, Jamaica, 2015,
I encounter Lincoln –  downtrodden, but fighting –
on every crossing;
I see Phibbah

in women who find freedom in men;
Susannah in the Ananda Alerts
of missing boys and girls;
I  see the surviving chattels of the Egypt plantation
in the black-or-white-suited mourners
of the recently gunned-down area youth,

And I wonder
*Who in Thistlewood's diary would I have been?*

## PHILIP, AN EXCELLENT FISHERMAN

Was there nowhere to sail to,
or were you only a fisherman
in bracketed waters,
the plantations your parenthesis?

Oh Philip, excellent fisherman
in this "Slaves for Sale"
I saw on the Internet, but applicable first
on Monday, 18th May, 1829,
when the plantation, in hard times,
advertised its slaves for hire,

did you ever find somewhere
apart from the recesses of your mind
to sail to?

# DRAWING

The emancipation declaration
is posted on a palm tree
that reaches for the sky.

Shackles are being dropped in a grave;
a boy's whole body grins
as he shovels them in.

A woman on a bench,
a bible beside her,
offers her baby to the sky.

A whip – a dead snake –
lies under the feet of the man
with a jubilant face, jubilant hands.

A girl is on her knees
in witness to the shackle burial
and the celebration.

Behind these
the plantation is sketched
at Canboulay.

As the canefields burn,
all hands off deck
jouvay in jubilant air.

There's a ship,
distant, unrigged, skeletal,
that squats, like memory, on the sea.

## SSO MUCH THINGS TO SAYS

We agreed to talk through poems –
you in Africa, me in Jamaica.

Should genealogy prove your forebears rob I,
sold I into violence that is sewn like cane
into the landscape,
into babymodda, babyfaddahood,
the house vs field slave continuum,
do I & I insist on reparations from you, too,
brodda in Africa?

Or is play I playing fool –
ignoring Cain, Jacob and Esau
an de one dem who sell out Garvey fi rice?

# TUNNELS & ECHOES

I

We approach a tunnel, and when
we're in, my head swivels to the light.
When I lose sight of it,
I shut my eyes and hope for sleep,
bury my head in Randold's arm.

I fear dark spaces, like tunnels,
like ram-packed coaster buses,
I explain on my way to Merida
where tunnels cut through mountains.

II

We came over in blackness
darker than any I fear being trapped in,
darker than the marrow this memory tunnels.

III

In dark spaces time collapses
travels back…

# GRANMAMMY

Granmammy's mammy was a Puerto Rican
an' as Granmammy sey
her daddy was a true blood
Coromantine man.

Granmammy sey
I remin' her of her Puerto Rican mammy
de way I 'tan' infront di mirror an' fix mi hair
like so an' so.

She use to sey: *Is same way so*
*yu great granmammy use' to 'tan*
*wid' 'ar likkle likkle wais', an 'ar long, long, hair;*
*infront di mirror, a fix 'ar face.*

Granmammy's mammy was a Puerto Rican
an' as Granmammy sey
her daddy was a true blood
Coromantine man.

An' when my granmammy come from foreign,
she sit an' spin, an' pedal  de sewing machine,
mek skirt an' frock an' blouse
fi 'ar likkle Coromantine, quarter Chinese
Puerto Rican gal.

# LEAVES

It's November, autumn in China;
I'm on the bus watching
an old man raking leaves.
As they fall, he collects them,

so no leaf stays long enough
for you to remember it
there on the road.

What stays is the old man raking leaves;
collecting them as they fall.

And I think I see why Popo,
who hopped the boat
from China to the island,
rakes leaves, morning, evening.

## POPO

The sky is telling its grief,
Popo. For five nights it pours.
How long will it last – you away half the year?

You perched at the window
my entire walk home from school,
remember?

Your skirt was my armour
from duppies, strangers and my father
on the days his eyes were red.

The sky is telling its grief,
Popo. I sleep and dream of you;
we're raking leaves in the yard.

## CHA & MEECHANG

There's a Chinese girl in pantaloons
pouring out cha
on the bone china tea set;
she reminds me of you, Popo,
making cha in the morning.

There were times you'd stand
in front of the stove
and make meechang:
boiling the sugar with lime juice
till it was a sticky syrup.

You'd pour it on the bed of Rice Krispies
and roller-pinned peanuts
laid out on greaseproof paper,
then wait for it to set
to cut it into squares.

Popo, as I sip Bojenmi tea
from the Egret River brand,
I imagine now the two of us
in a ritual of cha and meechang.

## AFTER TANGSHAN

Outside the museum,
staring at the bone-grey recalling wall
etched with the names of thousands lost,

it hits me, like the pain
of not knowing my mother
– that old tsunami in my blood.

# MEMORIES

The last time I saw her
in person, not a photograph,
she was in the box beside me
in Cleopatra braids
popping gumballs in the cinema.

I called my stepmother mommy
and she said: *Tell her*
*you have only one mother,* **me,**
*and* **she** *is Aunty M.*

At the table, at dinnertime,
I delivered the message.
My father delivered
chopsticks to my forehead.

She'd call from Venezuela,
and I'd pack bags, and wait for her.

I remember the barrel
with the biggest doll I'd ever seen.

I remember nights without a mother.

# CARD

The green silk bow with the white stars of David
is glittered and plump,
hiding the neck of the blue-eyed, glitter-nose pup
under the glittered mistletoe and red berries
on a glittered Santa hat.

There are presents on the floor
wrapped and ribboned with silk,
one held by a Christmas mouse-elf
with its little pink toes,
red jacket, red Santa hat
and a cherry-red nose.

You sent me this card from Venezuela;
on the inside: *From Mom*,
three lines of Spanish: no *amor* dropped in
something about *Navidad, Prospero Año*
and then a line from you: *all the best wishes*.

I refinger this card at thirty-seven
and remember how I hated Spanish class
since *amor* was nowhere,
how I stood in the crib of the matchbox house
we shared until I was three,
before you left for Venezuela
and I moved in with my father.

## THE WOULD-BE-LINES

*Why bother,* I said to her,
she dressed casually, walking
into the office where
they dress to the T.
So naturally I thought she was visiting.

*Excuse me?* she gave me.
*Aren't you on leave?* I gave her.

*My mother died,*
*and I'm coming in to apply for it now,*
she gave me back.

And what of my mother,
as time strangles the would-be-
lines between us?

Will I have to say goodbye to her
without ever saying something
like: *Mom, mi talk to yu lata*
*yu grandawta, she mekking a mess.*

## AT SEA

I drift in a vulnerable craft
and write mother poems at sea.

She's the flounder that escapes
my handmade fishing rod,

so I weave a net at night
from the three memories I have of her.

And I'm just seeing it now – no, not
the picture of a dead Sylvia Plath

half out of the oven,
no, not that

but the similarity,
the obsession.

I write mother poems at sea,
drift and hope for her,

but then, my daughter –
the anchor.

# VENEZUELA JOURNAL

At the back of the plane
on the way to Venezuela
the tail dips, the wings swing
as the bird battles mountain and wind.
I think: Did she think of me, as I of her
at the back of the plane
on the way to Venezuela?

The first morning, I sit at the window,
look out for her, and write
as bikes, cars, people navigate the road.

Did she leave that man by the window
standing there in his *apartamento*,
like a statue, looking down?
Is he too searching faces for hers?
Will she be the help coming in to change *el bebé*
in another *apartamento* I look right into
from the 10<sup>th</sup> floor of the Hotel Alex?

*¿Madre mía, donde estás?*

The clouds lift from the mountains
in the la Candalaria area of Caracas.
Birds gather on roofs, then
soar above human conditions.

You are the cloud, mi madre, ghostlike.

Two hundred years back in a rented room
in downtown Kingston,
Simón Bolívar penned *la Carta de Xaymaica*.
Today I sit at the window in the Hotel Alex,
sip Jamaican rum from the bottle

hit letters on the keyboard
and look down to see mi madre
in every brown-skinned woman
passing on the road.

# SPILT

Randold and I scoop up the spilt contents
of the plastic bag before the light
turns green and cars in Merida,
like cars in Kingston,
make cats of us and spill our guts.

I am the bag,
my mother the contents that spill
on the road of Venezuela –
the country she left me for.

# RAGDOLL

Randold, my guide in Venezuela, saw your text:
*Mommy, how many things have you bought me so far?*
went and bought you the ragdoll you've since named Jessica,
a smaller companion to Abigail –
the ragdoll I bought you for being good at the dentist –
the doll you share a bed with, tea parties,
the car, the swing, the hammock in the yard.
You held her in the hospital
all the time your great-grandmother was dying.

In the car today, your grand auntie tells you how
as a girl they made me up, sashed me
Mini Miss Jamaica, snapped me. There was another
with my hair in an afro – hands out to the east and west,
fingers spread like a dancer in a pose, in a long,
floral print, paper-cut-out-fringed-skirt – their ragdoll.

Now there's you.
And from the first time I noticed how
your hands reach into the morning,
I knew I wanted to live
and Plath was no longer romantic.
From the first time I held you and saw that blue pout
morph into a wail, you subsumed all ragdolls,
as we weave invisible silk around us.

## DI DREAM

Yu was infront de mirror, fixing up
wid two men in de room.
Ah doan' waan say it was a dressing room
an dem yu goons, 'cause, though
yu have eyes dat would mesmerize de worl'
ah doan want dat for yu.
Is like de siren always die early,
de pearl always slip t'rough de hands
back to de scatterbrain sea
when de whole worl' want one woman.

Yu looked 18 or 19, de age when
a girl is a clear glass of water.
Yu was talking to dem, like yu know
how to handle men.
Was like glimpsing de future
'cause ah look straight in yu eyes
an' yu never see mi.

But dat was den, an' ah hope since ah eat
an' drink some'ting, an' talk it, it woan' happen.
'Cause, ah doan waan yu wake from yu sleep, crying
in de sheet for yu modda.
Ah doan waan *yu* walk roun' in mystery an' a-wonda.

# #10 HIALEAH

In the days when rain was unexplained
and magical, the bogey man
would materialize in the downpour
and I'd spy through the window.

Junior, across the road, would pick green cherries,
gulp them for power, and I'd follow,
as I followed cousin Maurice who insisted
I spurt spider-web from my palms
to climb down the lime tree.
I still have the scar on my elbow.
And though I cut my leg on the fence
going over next door, I never saw
the old woman I heard calling:
*Who dere, who dere?*

At the high school up the road
a man sold gum-cigarettes at the gate.
In the evenings, he'd padlock up,
cycle home with pants in his socks,
in the days when rain was unexplained
and magical.

# YESTERDAY

Once I gulped a container of pills
wishing to never come back
to a room, a house without my mother.

The day after, searching for something
in my eyes as he put the glass of milk
to my lips, my father asked:
*Why did you do it?*

I could only look at him.

# DADDY

I'm up with the consumptive moon,
the image of Keats convulsing to death,
and the memory of you, after your father died,
charging into the room where I had hung
the greaseproof paper and bamboo fish
he made me, with his own hands,
that travelled from China.

You dragged it down, like a hideous painting,
flung it on the heap in the yard,
doused it with kerosene, lit it
and stood there as it burned.
I stood, unseen, behind you
watching you burn the one thing I had of him.

And yet, Daddy, only you knew
to get me the red, remote control sports car,
the neat, cream and brown sneakers,
the zipper jacket –
white, to Michael Jackson's red.

We spent hours in front of the TV
watching Ali, Joe Frazier, Sugar Ray.

I understudied you, Daddy,
with your boxing heroes, your fast cars,
your tending of hurts
like a garden of night-blooming cereus,
angel trumpets, red ixorias.

I know how to let people go
like ribbons in the wind.

# AT THE KARAOKE BAR, 21ST CENTURY HOTEL

I sit at the bar in the 21$^{st}$ Century Hotel
Beijing, drinking cheap Chinese liquor.
The room is dark, full of smoke, with a song
scrolling on the screen I crane my neck to follow.
There's a man. Girls look into his eyes
as he caresses the mic and sings.

His song stops and a girl takes the mic
and he floats over to me and says:
*You're very pretty,* orders me American whisky.
And I remember you, Daddy,
telling me how your parents shipped you off at six
to Canton, to know your culture.

I remember you playing the harmonica,
the banjo, singing Chinese opera,
telling me stories of being brown in China,
being loved by a Chinese stepmother;
of girls intrigued by an oval face,
long brown limbs and massive waves of hair;
of being the village basketball star.

I remember how we talked
and think: tomorrow I'll pack
the Mao cap, Chinese cigarettes,
Fung Fung Yen, Fa Chung for my daddy.

# THE SCORE

*The gods may throw a dice*
*their minds as cold as ice*
*and someone way down here*
*loses someone dear.*

— ABBA

Death came dressed
as an inattentive nurse
dispatching you at the window
for pneumonia to blow its breath in
on you, a man at 80.

I've raged since, at the nurse,
the world of dying.
I scored it 12-1. Yours the first loss,
a grandpa stolen.

My daughter, the first victory
– a seedling growing.

## BROTHER

At nine, I pick flowers for your birthday,
wishing you were playing in the garden, or on
the verandah, taking the ladders off the fire truck,
arranging them to rescue
the child trapped in the room.

At seventeen, I come home from the mission tent,
clutching the hope of a miracle
like a crystal in my hand that drops
and splinters when I see you – still
as you were before the crusade.

At twenty-four, I stand in the morgue
of the hospital you were born in.
They screwed up, again: a girl shares
your cold chamber. But I resent more
your botched delivery.

Norvin, when you died, I walked in a whirlwind.
Your father? Glass splintered, senseless,
barring me and your mother from the cremation.
For more than a year your mother
seemed obsessed with ovens:
putting in the beginnings of puddings, pies
tarts; taking them out completed.

Sometimes I see you, once in a boy
at a school I taught – the same living hair
cut close to the scalp, the same smile.
Norvin, my brother, I kiss your black brow
and wish my world was like my daughter's
where a tear drop would bring you back.

## MENELEK

If I close my eyes and concentrate,
erase the pencilling on the page that says you die
like rain washes off the chalk
children mark on driveways,
maybe you would not have been murdered
at the junction – the blasted bus stop
of young black men's lives.

Maybe you'd still be Menelek, the boy
with the dreads and Incient spirit
I lifted across the rocks
in the river at Caymanas,
years ago when I was young
and your death already written,

and my curse already proven.

# DIANA

*You prepare for one sorrow,*
*but another comes.*
*It is not like the weather,*
*you cannot brace yourself...*
                    — Derek Walcott

I could paint my toenails red
for some red-hot fling
since it's summer when all bells ring.
Then again, I could leave them sans polish.
You never know what that may bring.

I could wear Auntie Diana's Anne Carson pretty
silk-lined, polyester blouse with shades of pink
and white flowers with orange centres,
arches of green stems, shouts of leaves,
with asymmetrical, ruffled sleeves – like petals
when I want to just be free.

I could remember not to laugh too loud;
to avoid cats, 'specially if they're black.
Then again you can never do that, can you:
ward things off, prepare for them, like death,
who walked one day, straight into Uncle Neville's life
took Auntie Diana, his wife?

How do you prepare for that?

## GIRL WITH MY FACE

I see you in the obituaries –
the girl my stepmother mistook for me
and blew the horn, 'cause 'I' saw her
and never came.

To see you, who the librarian thought
had already come for your report
when she saw me;
to see the girl with the bow legs I had,
but the voice for ballads I never did;
to see you, the girl with my face,
in the obituaries, jolts me.

I pray your parents never see my face.

# ANTI-HEROINE

I hated your death, Anna;
it felt false, written by a man:
the adulteress lays her neck on the track,
train comes and wham!
all mankind, cuckolded at least, revenged.

Might as well you did stone her,
like some people do,
or stab de whoring bitch, like Cosmic Don.

But Sylvia, you twisted it:
the cuckolded woman kills herself.
All I can say in self-deception is
that must have been written by the Daddy-god,
reaching for you through the grave.

# BEARING WITNESS

*for Mervyn Morris*

You search the water,
examine the life caught in the seine.

The first day you saw him –
the man whose father died
and his mother cried
and her tears were his –
your eyes opened wide.

He conjured a pond
in your exam, long before
you came to know how poetry stands,
travels far, burrows deeply.

His white beard jabbed the corner
before his blue jeans, doctor's shirt
and the stars in his eyes seized the room,
transfixed by his baritone that dipped to bass
like a bucket, plunged into the depths of Mervyn,
then surfaced with overflowing laughter.

And the class, on the edge, drew near
as he led us down the dark
red lanes of Martin Carter;
sat with us around the Singer sewing machine
of Lorna Goodison's mother.

He'd used Bay Rum
to clean the Mikey Smith cassette head
so we'd hear the Legba-walking,
Orange-Street-fire-talking man
dem kill wid a stone on Stony Hill.
Him plug dat radio stuck inna

Jean Binta Breeze head into fi wi,
an' walk wi on de street wid Oku,
Linton, Muta, wid him patty pan.

An' when him talk serious 'bout Miss Lou
di class on di edge draw nearer
an' we peered into de pool.

It was Mervyn Morris who inflicted
the love pangs of John Donne
and W.B. Yeats upon us,
bringing life from the depths of souls
to his class, which was never
contained on the Mona Campus.

He was already Poet Laureate.

His progeny? Many.

So I, manuscript in hand
like generations of others,
negotiate the wet summer, the lush grass,
the paths to Mervyn Morris –
tennis-ball poem bouncer,
Rhodes Scholar, wry quicksilver star-eye,
Don Drummond fan,
generous magic-poem-man –
the fathomless pond.

So, how do you bear witness?
You search the water,
examine the life in the seine,
commit every detail,
then, slip them back in,
roll your world back up to a scroll,
unfold it, breathe, begin.

# THE ARTIST

*"If I could afford it, I would buy that work from the government
and call it* The Singing Poet." — *Christopher Gonzalez*

Can you tell a man not to feel
the sting of rejection
after he used himself up
in tribute to Marley
the legend he saw as a tree?

Can you tell him he saw shit;
you want legs, not a trunk,
and not expect him to leave your city
for the trees, the sea and the riva mumma
pond in Runaway Bay, St. Ann?

When I met Christopher Gonzalez,
the riva mumma's face he'd seen in the pond
not far from his home in St. Ann, and in his dreams,
was on every neck on every canvas in his studio.
I believe he married her,
though her river hands didn't remove the clouds
from his eyes, guarding the words he uttered
as we pulled on our spliffs on the beach,
drew sustenance from the sea
and engaged the red head Liz.

When I pass the same beach –
that now only hotel guests can access –
I imagine your Marley, still rising from the roots,
in Island Village, St. Ann,
picking "Redemption Song", chanting down Babylon
with your river mumma companion, in harmony.

# SHELL

It was white and swirled
like any other snow-mountain shell,
with still a bit of dirt in it
from the slug that once lived there
recently evacuated.
At least, that's what Stephan said,
who gave me the shell –
Stephan Marsh Planchart,
the hermit poet of Merida,
who makes papers in the mountains
and strums his guitar,
lightning shooting from his head.
I understood the gift,
closed my hand around it.

Back home in Red Hills,
the family got sick, blamed my shell.
After all, upheavals happen when two worlds meet,
and fearing us vulnerable like the Tainos,
I wrapped the shell in a plastic bag, dumped it.

Now, I look on the shelf where the shell was
and see it there, like any other swirling shell
in the white mountains of Merida, Venezuela.
And I see Stephan with his guitars and lightning-bolt hair
in the middle of Marley's "Satisfy My Soul"
crooning *Oh please don't you rock my boat…*

# AND THERE'S ROBERT

Like a brother,
the way we take the world and make it
our own big ball.

When he regales me with tales of his dives,
of the magic city laying herself bare
right after rain, and he seeing so much skin
and a belly button like the X on a map
of a treasure isle; of the attack of the lionfish,
the rusty metal on the seafloor,
I see his Port Royal head shake and gesticulate
and the stars in his pupils twinkle.

When he tells of his romance with the treacherous sea
and his sleeping beauty of a city, I see myself
and poetry, how it bites, like his lionfish,
his rusting metal on the seafloor;
yet we keep going back to it,
convinced life lies in its undulating fathoms.

KINGSTON BUTTERCUP

# THE WARNER WOMAN ON PORT ROYAL

*for Eddie Baugh*

*Revelation 18 vs 21:*

On de sea dem buil' a town!
In a flash, it get suck down!

Two t'ousan' drown!

O God! when de' great eart' quake
Port Royal drop to it knee!

People float like ants, as
when yu spray ants' hole wid hose!

An' two t'ousan' dead from sickness!

Yu fi gi' Caesar what 'im due
but fin' yu knees!

before Great God stamp one foot down!
an' di whole ah yu drown!

# DEAR CESAR VALLEJO...

*Mr. Minister of Health: what to do?*
*Ah, unfortunately, human men,*
*there is, brothers, much too much to do.*
— Cesar Vallejo

Dear Cesar Vallejo,

in Jamaica, our collective anger is like the sea;
it undulates, then goes under
like a nine-day-wonder;
or somehow straightens out
like the crushes of waves that flatten
into nothingness, like cloth ironed smooth.

So my grandmother is a dead fish,
an unknown, uncounted statistic,
whose heart couldn't survive the viruses'
rampage, on a body gone eighty-one,
but until then strong.

My grandmother, transplanted from China,
was thrown under the bus, like the rest of us,
who never knew how susceptible we were.
Since mum was the word, the people
lacked knowledge and perished!

So, in Jamaica, Mr. Vallejo,
government stands at the board
like a silent god in heaven
above the crinkled cloth,
and the cloth whose anger is ironed smooth, is us.

## TAP

It's Sunday, our water day.
Since the drought
it's water on alternate days,
but, not yet midday, the tap drains.

As the sea creeps in
and the earth heats up,
plagues and fear of them scatter –
like the gold film of dust above Kingston
they say is from the Sahara;
like the tree-gobbling fires in Stony Hill, Gordon Town;
like the rumour, *The robots will take over.*

# RED HILLS

The underground spring in Red Hills
flows through Plantation Heights
into a river in Caymanas.

It tells of a murdered landlord,
left to float in the almost secret
mineral spring boys in the area sea-kick in;
of the gunman, Sandokan,
what he ate, what he thought,
camping out, on the run;
when bullets clap night.

The underground spring of my hill
tells of blood seeping down its side,
man – a wounded bird – on its shoulder.

## SHAKER WAY

Good Friday,
you wake to a car
stolen from your neighbour's driveway.

Saturday, a man lurks in the shadows
in the middle of Shaker Way, near the car
that squats in front of the house on its right.
You know he could be
mapping the scene, plotting the act,
tying you up in your home,
boxing your face, taking more than money.

You know there could be yellow tape.

## SEA DIRGE

Went to the beach,
searched the horizon,
its blue fading to white;

saw the seagulls,
the ritual of fish and festival;

saw a man
walking on the moss-covered-rocks
to disappear into a lean-to on the beach

– blood-soaked shirt peeled,
fresh chop to his chest.

# MISSING

Had gone to look for the man
who sold fruits by the road,
the stretch before Gordon Town
and the cool rivers that flow –
well, one river, really, that flows
on different shoulders
of the many-shouldered-hill.

Had gone to reminisce, perhaps,
at the very least, to stand
on his concrete and look down
and around at Kintyre below,
the neighbourhood of deep
green trees and sky above.

But, *'Im go farm
an' dem kill 'im
an' bury 'im*

his son had to surmise.

# MARGINAL

## I

Likkle help go a long way sometime,
like di Red Stripe, firs' ting Saturday
fi mek yu buckle up, an' buckle down
to wipe de boutique shop display window clean;
feed di plants dem wata; vacuum di rug
ready up di place fi de boss
an' di woman dem, wid boutique store money.

## II

Cassandra D had a typewriter inna de tenement
to teach she neighbours how to read an' write,
an' shed some light, in di election year.

One night, dem mash it up
go een pon 'ar, an t'reaten:
*If yu kip one more meeting we come back fi yu. Hear?*

An' dere were witnesses on de bed
in de one-room-tenement:
de son from ar uncle, de girl she adop'.

Cassandra D doan live inna de tenement no more.
'Ar fadda, once los', den found, now dead,
buy a house to ease de pain.

III

De night before de nine night
mi bawl in de lane
wail for 'im soul.

An' at de wake
mi aim de gun to de sky
an' fire.

# KINGSTON BUTTERCUP

I

A girl hops off the bus from school
in Arlene Gardens.

A driver, with the car full of children,
commandeers her eyes

– erect cock in hand.


II

You see Tamara on Red Hills Road
or Half-Way-Tree
in tight clothes – sometimes weave,
sometimes wig –

her jaguar-black skin
and her eyes hooking yours
as she weaves through cars,
puts out hand and begs.

Her voice and polite words
are pleasing,
but behind her eyes
you see a jaguar reeling.


III

*If a bad man dem a fuck*
*or a police, mi no care,*
*mi ready fi dead!*

blasts the windscreen cleaner at the stoplight
at the intersection of Hope Road
and Half Way Tree, before he starts
chanting in an unknown language.


IV

There's a detour just before the KFC
on Red Hills Road –
the third for the month.
Yellow tape and cops indicate
another taxi man who didn't pay his dues,
or businessman feeling him balls
an' refusing to pay di protection money,
or just one more loader man who chat too much
in dis bloody city.


V.

Before the Ganja Commission free up
two ounce a weed,
a Rastaman sight Babylon on Red Hills Road
an' drop him spliff.
But too late; dem see an stop 'im.


VI.

The bike man rides head on,
flings obscenities into the car.
I dash them back at him.
He turns, starts chasing.
I floor the '99 Levin.

VII

Monday morning there's the usual snake,
inching up exhaust-filled Molynes with the sun,
narrating this story from before the Tainos.
Then yellow seduces your dead-ahead
eyes on the road, and you see
Kingston buttercups restrained by the sidewalk
on your left. They hold you like that;
you feel your pulse relax, your grip
on the wheel loosen, you, floating…

# NIGHT-BLOOMING CEREUS

*for Kwame Dawes*

Each time I unlock the grill to the morning
and wade through the growing crab grass,
the night-blooming cereus with its ghostlike
white petals and mysterious bouquet
is already spent,
already done with this world
and its grilled fretwork.

So, I put this one in my room
and when it blooms, I shove
my daughter's nose in it:
*Smell it, smell it, Kayla;*
*it's the night-blooming cereus*!

And for the entire night
she has to be fed oxygen through a mask,
and I am hauled through a needle at the hospital,
as I see up-close the venom
of beauty lying under the skin.

## ANOTHER SEASON

Walcott was right:
it is the season of phantasmal peace
in the evening, when birds usher in
a change in time;

when they lift the shadow of day
with a crease of light
where night begins its downward crawl,
like a spider descending your sky-patterned curtain.

And in the morning, when the birds
lift the net of shadows,
a full-band, orchestrated show
they've practised day-in, day-out for,
your day announces
another season of phantasmal peace.

# EVE AND THE SNAKE, 2012

You must know how poinsettias
glow for Christmas with their red velvet leaves
and gold-bulb jingle bells.

With your prowling 'round gardens for centuries
you've probably seen this a million times –
a woman pruning poinsettias, a stem waiting
beside her to be planted to bloom for December.

Perhaps you expected that when I'd seen you
I'd drop the garden tools on the way over
to my daughter and her father,
who delight in things like you.

Perhaps you knew he'd try to catch you,
so you disappeared in a fissure in the wall
so quickly, it chopped your tail off –

your tail that now wriggles
on the white plane of memory.

# GUINEA-HEN WEED

I smell of guinea-hen weed today –
green like the weed my feet trample;
the weed dogs toss and roll their heads in,
in frenzied, happy, dog-gestures.

I smell of guinea-hen weed today:
I drank the tea so maybe I'll find
an open window and toss my fingers through,
and they'll root in the ground,
sprout guinea-hen leaves.

# WHITE POUI

Footsteps from my home,
they chop you down –
prune really –
but for the waiting time
till you're a fountain again
it's a vicious butchering,
a drought, where I pray God
anxiously for your re-springing.

# JULIE

Dis big-bottom Julie remin' mi
of a sweetie-come-brush-mi mango tree
on de lawn of de house on Sunnyfiel' Drive
in Havendale, when summer mango de air;

it remin' mi of after school, sucking a hairy
till it grey; of a low limb dat yu sit on like a jockey,
wid' Julie mango juice running dung yu han'
quicker dan yu tongue can stop i'.

Dis big-bottom-Julie infront mi
mek de min' tink all dese t'ings –
but mos' to jus' grab i', an' nyam  i'.

# ROCK

So why dem really chop de penis
from offa de cliff?
Man fi look pon pum rock
an' ooh and ahh,
but non ah dat fi ooman?

Sorry mi neva aks Portia fi buil'
back de tool pan de cliff
fi we de ooman dem have
somet'in fi ooh and aah ova.

On the almost opposite side of the road from Pum Rock in Bog Walk Gorge
was an outcrop that looked slightly like a penis. This did not generate as much
interest as Pum Rock, however. Unfortunately, the penis rock was slowly cut
away as it was proving to be hazardous to passing vehicles…

# IMMERSE

My hands duck the grey
and black dress
three times in the water
before I hold it
and scrub it with the brush.

After that comes the ritual
*scritch, scritch, scritch*
to free it of signs
of the rub a dub I still hanker after

in a smouldering room
with boom boxes, and a man
pinned to this grey and black dress
that when accessorized with a pink
snake-skin belt, skirts middle thigh.

# AND THESE TWO

*Them*

August, sunset on summer:
a 14-year-old labours in the ward,
delivers a son to the garrison.

The man, 22, will lavish kicks,
kisses on his first born.

*Him*

At 14 he'd already *known* the sitters;
followed his mom to work in the clubs.

At 16, the hop-scotch-job-game:
landscape artist, delivery/taximan.
*Anyting yu want, him dat.*

*Her*:

In Jamaica, where nothing is secret,
she moved in at three with her dad,
his Chinese wife and family.

Teachers called her *Jacket*
since the Chinese wife insisted
the black girl was hers.

She felt like the runt of the clowns
ejected from the vehicle,
sprayed with a water-gun-flower
so the entire circus crowd
would peel with laughter.

*Them*:

He saw her from where he stood
in a beach shed at Hellshire.

No sound but the waves,
a cay and its coconuts,
a dark sea warm as breath,
black pebbles scuttling up,
black pebbles washing back.

And these two, cradled
by the tide, in each other.

No sound but the waves…

And there was that time in the car:
the music – right;
the language – lucid.

# PEENY WALLY

*Female peenie wallies do not have wings.*

I

Nearly six in the evening,
the river darkens.
There are peenie wallies,
men auctioning wings –
to the woman with the sweetest mouth,
the most dazzling lights.

And there are times, it seems, I get your wings,
times, it seems, you take them back.

II

Midnight, New Year,
I'm on the balcony with you
watching peenie wallies –
luminous bodies electrifying night,
the upcoming year, with promises.

# DOMESTIC: A DIPTYCH

*Love is never any better than the lover.*
—Toni Morrison, *The Bluest Eye*

I

Light blue sky, white clouds,
a Westmoreland Sunday ruled by sun;
five steps down from the road, children,
grown-ups arranged at the seas' hem
in the sand-carpet;
houses on both sides of the road,
a patch of land – grass overgrown;
a woman and a man.

She goes down, gets up,
goes down again. His hands,
feet deliver blows.
A house looks up
intermittently from the paper.

II

Going down Red Hills I see him:
travelling bag at foot,
another bag stuffed like a teddy
under his arm
at a corner where buses and taxis pause.

If you didn't know
of men beating their women,
then retreating with bags,
you'd never think
on seeing him at the corner
that perhaps this was one of them.

# MIRROR

I've seen the bud become a flower.

She accessorized in me
with colours and jewellery
then switched off lights, left.

I could have reflected her fatter,
but remembering the girl before –
how she too budded and blossomed
into a bloom who forgot me,
I softened, kept my reflections true.

But one day, she *was* fatter
and she wasn't disturbed, just smiled
with curved hand under her belly.

Then she brought a baby to me
started singing: *Who's that pretty girl
in the mirror there?*

For seasons the little girl smiled at me,
then, one day when she was three,
examined her outfit and winked.

Today, my concern is the girl who grew
in my reflection. The girl who touches the side
of her face, following the raised curve
like a red sickle moon;

the girl who examines her ear
and tries to hold the sobs.

# BUSTED EARDRUM

*Give it six weeks, it should heal,* Doc says.
For the next six weeks, she's the girl
who walks with night in her ear,
right there in her left ear
every waking, sleeping day.
Rumbling, tumbling, varooming
big booming vehicles echo
in her ear. For a hurtling second
she'll be superhero, with tunnel hearing,
capable of holding a sound longer
than most anyone –
the water tilting in a drinking glass
an ocean roaring in her ear.

## SINCE YOU'VE BEEN GONE

my midnights have been busy.
I may need a roster
for the supporting men
and their guest appearances,
for the varied places I go to at nights;

the twists that dream me – the great writer plots:
the episodes of car stuck in a rut,
me taking it up like the Flintstones –
my feet, the wheels
that go round and round;

Yes, since you've been gone,
my midnights have been busy.

## CHEATED

The earth, the headstones, my white
shoes were red. I think even my white net
stockings were red. And the clouds
that would have been my father's heart
and his brothers', I imagine were red
that day at the cemetery
when we put *Jagung* down.

My father and his father had cold and hot
currents between them. But when Jagung died
and I stood at his grave, I felt (even at ten)
that *this was a cheat;*
I was meant to have more of him.

Now when I keep a distance
as you play with our daughter
the feeling of *being cheated* creeps in.

# REBEL

A man lures a dog into his yard with bacon.
He gets his penis bittten right off
when he tries to shove it in the dog's ass –

an image for the beginnings of revolution
when the downpressed fight back,
like Marlon James' night women

who enact revenge on the plantation.
But then there's our farm workers in foreign
sent back-a-yaad when injured on the job.

There's Ananda Dean who was kidnapped
and murdered. And there's Marley
who said *Rebel!*

# ENDNOTES

p. 14, "On Reading Thistlewood's Diary". *Ananda Alert*: Ananda Morgan was kidnapped in 2010 and her body found weeks after. The Ananda Alert, whereby a bulletin is given from a Police Station to the public when a child has gone missing, was named so in 2011. *Egypt* was the name of Thistlewood's plantation in Westmoreland.

p. 16, "Drawing". The poem references a drawing entitled *Full Freedom 1838*. It comes from Richard Robert Madden's book, *A Twelvemonth's Residence in the West Indies, during the transition from slavery to apprenticeship; with incidental notice of the state of society, prospects, and natural resources of Jamaica and other islands* (Philadelphia: Carey, Lea and Blanchard, 1835)

p. 20, "Popo". *Popo*: Hakka Chinese dialect for grandma.

p. 36, "At the Karaoke Bar". *Fung Fung Yen*: biscuits; *Fa Chung*: sausage.

p. 42, "Anti-Heroine". *Cosmic Don*: a reference to the great Jamaican trombonist, Don Drummond, who in a state of mental disturbance murdered his partner and died in a mental hospital.

p. 45, "The Artist", quote from an interview with Gonzalez by Lim in 2004.

p. 56, "Sea Dirge". *Festival*: a Jamaican culinary delicacy made from flour, cornmeal, salt, sugar and baking powder, fried till golden.

p. 61, "Kingston Buttercup". *Loader man*: person (usually a man) who gets a small cut when he "loads" taxis with passengers.

p. 71, "And These Two". *Jacket*: term given to a child whose paternity is in question, especially when the child does not have enough features of the father.

p. 78, "Cheated". *Jagung*: Hakka Chinese dialect for grandfather.

# ABOUT THE AUTHOR

Ann-Margaret Lim lives in Red Hills, Jamaica.

Her critically praised first collection of poems, *The Festival of Wild Orchid*, which was published by Peepal Tree Press in 2012, was nominated for the UK Guardian First Book prize and received Honorary Mention in the 2013 Bocas Prize.

Ann-Margaret, who was commissioned to write the ode for Jamaican Poet Laureate, Mervyn Morris, "Bearing Witness", which she read at the Kings House inauguration ceremony, was one of two Jamaican poets (the other being Morris) featured in the 2014 *Ebony Magazine* article: "Six Caribbean Writers to Discover this Summer".

She lives in appreciation of the mentorship from Wayne Brown, Mervyn Morris, Eddie Baugh, Kwame Dawes, Olive Senior, and the ground-breaking examples of Caribbean greats such as Derek Walcott and the current generation of Loretta Colins Klobah and Safiya Sinclair.

## ALSO BY ANN-MARGARET LIM

*The Festival of Wild Orchid*
ISBN: 9781845232016; pp. 80; pub. 2012; price £8.99

Here are poems alert to contemporary Jamaica in all its contradictions. Lyric and musical poems find fresh things to say about the beauties of landscape, sea shores, the joys and pains of love, and the novelty of the world as discovered by a young child.

Poems of pungent phrase and arresting image respond frankly to the poverty, sharp social divisions, endemic violence and misogyny that blight Jamaican lives. Written in both standard Caribbean English and Jamaican patois, the poems reveal an engaging poetic persona, feisty and questioning, who sees her world with wit and insight. The shaping of that persona is explored in poems that reflect on a Chinese and African Jamaican heritage and on experiences good and bad. Ann-Margaret Lim brings an individual vision to her observations, so her Jamaica is both recognisable and new.

"A significant first collection, shaping sympathy and indignation. It presents alert responses to social disparity, love, death and the natural world. It commemorates ancestors, mothers, artists, mentors and the ineffable, 'sprinkling / the dust of poems'."

— MERVYN MORRIS